THE CHANGING FACE OF
KENYA

Text by ROB BOWDEN
Photographs by CHRIS FAIRCLOUGH

HODDER
Wayland

an imprint of Hodder Children's Books

© 2002 White-Thomson Publishing Ltd

Produced for Hodder Wayland by
White-Thomson Publishing Ltd
2/3 St Andrew's Place
Lewes BN7 1UP

Editor: Anna Lee
Designer: Clare Nicholas
Concept design: Christopher Halls at Mind's Eye Design, Lewes
Proofreader: Jason Hook

First published in Great Britain in 2002 by Hodder Wayland, an imprint
of Hodder Children's Books.

British Library Cataloguing in Publication Data
Bowden, Rob
  The Changing Face of Kenya
  1. Kenya – Juvenile literature
  I. Title II. Kenya
  967.6′2′042

  ISBN: 0 7502 3991 3

Printed in Hong Kong by Wing King Tong Co. Ltd.

Hodder Children's Books
A division of Hodder Headline Limited,
338 Euston Rd, London NW1 3BH

Acknowledgements
The publishers would like to thank
the following for their contributions
to this book: Rob Bowden – statistics
panel research; Nick Hawken –
statistics panel illustrations on
pages 6, 19, 24, 30, 43, 44; Peter Bull –
map illustration on page 5. All
photographs are by Chris Fairclough
except: Rob Bowden 11 (bottom), 12,
32 (top); Steve White-Thomson
7 (top), 16 (bottom), 26, 28 (bottom),
35 (bottom).

Contents

Naivasha: a Town in Bloom

Resting in Kenya's Great Rift Valley is the small town of Naivasha. It lies next to a beautiful lake of the same name, and below a sleeping volcano called Mount Longonot. The combination of fertile soils, a plentiful supply of water and year-round sun and warmth make Naivasha perfect for growing a particularly lovely crop – flowers. Over the last ten years Kenya's flower industry has grown rapidly and Naivasha is at the centre of this dramatic change. Roses are the most valuable flowers grown but lilies and carnations are also popular varieties.

▲ *The Great Rift Valley stretches the entire length of Kenya. Flowers are just some of the crops grown here.*

Flower farming is the fastest growing industry in Kenya and is playing a lead role in the development of Kenya in many ways. Roads have been improved in order to transport the flowers more efficiently and new telecommunication systems allow growers to communicate with their overseas customers using e-mail and the Internet. Thousands of jobs have been created and many workers benefit from housing, health care and education facilities provided by the farms. However, there are also concerns about the impact of the farms on the Kenyan environment. Environmentalists are worried that flower farms use too much water from Lake Naivasha and that the chemicals used to grow flowers could pollute local water systems.

The development of Naivasha represents the many challenges confronting Kenya today. It must look for ways to build a strong economy to benefit its growing population, half of whom live in poverty. But it must also ensure that its rich and varied natural environment is protected from pollution and degradation.

▼ *Flower farms around Naivasha have created many new jobs.*

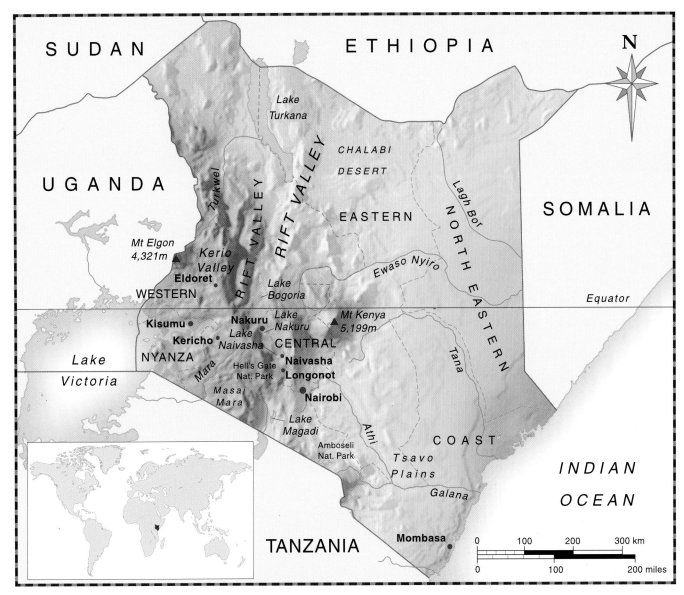

▲ *This map shows the places mentioned in this book and other major features of Kenya.*

KENYA: KEY FACTS

Area: 582,646 sq km

Population: 31.3 million (2001 estimate)

Population density: 54 people per sq km

Capital city: Nairobi (population 2.35 million in 1999)

Other main cities: Mombasa (0.7 million), Kisumu (0.3 million), Nakuru (0.25 million)

Highest mountain: Mt Kenya (5,199 m)

Longest river: Tana River (605 km)

Main languages: English, Swahili and around 200 other African languages

Major religions: Christianity (62%), traditional beliefs (30%), Islam (6%), others (2%)

Currency: Kenyan Shilling (100 cents = 1 Kenyan Shilling)

Past Times

Kenya became a British colony in the late nineteenth century, but by the mid-twentieth century many Kenyans were demanding the right to self-rule. After a series of violent clashes, the British began negotiations with Kenyan leaders and Kenya finally became independent in 1963. However, the influence of the colonial period is still very strong. English is the main language taught in Kenyan schools, for example, and many of Kenya's laws are based on the British legal system. Kenya's railways were also constructed by the British, who transported labourers from their Indian colony to build the rail network. Many of them stayed and today Indians are a very influential part of the Kenyan economy, running many of its biggest businesses.

One of the most lasting colonial influences is the pattern of land ownership. When the British and other Europeans arrived in Kenya they settled on the most productive farmland. Their descendants, many of them born in Kenya, still control large areas of this land today. The areas that returned to African control are owned by relatively few individuals. Most Kenyans have only small plots of land,

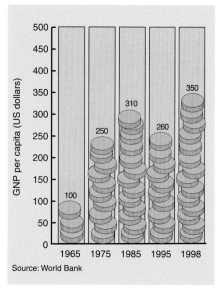

Source: World Bank

▲ *The Kenyan Gross National Product has increased significantly since 1965.*

◄ *This view of the old port in Mombasa, historically the gateway to Kenya, shows the city's combination of old and new architecture. The buildings in the foreground date from colonial times, while the high-rise blocks were constructed in the late twentieth century.*

or land that is of poorer quality and prone to soil erosion and water shortages.

Today, large farms produce cash crops for export to Europe and other markets in much the same way as they did during the colonial period. This pattern has tied Kenya into a heavy dependence on agricultural exports for its income. For example, tea and coffee account for around 30 per cent of Kenya's total export earnings. Because the value of agricultural produce varies dramatically on world markets, it can be difficult for Kenyans to plan their future with much certainty. Finding alternatives to these patterns of land ownership and production is one of the greatest challenges facing Kenyans today.

▲ *Tea, introduced to Kenya by the English, is now one of Kenya's main exports.*

IN THEIR OWN WORDS

'My name is Peter Melita and I work as a yard marshal for Kenya Railways. It is my job to control the trains as they are loaded or unloaded and pass through the station. I started working here in 1969 when I was just 19 years old and have been here for thirty-two years. In that time the railway has declined greatly. We used to have many trains transporting people and cargo all over Kenya. Now, the modern buses take passengers from Nairobi to Mombasa and lorries carry much of the cargo. We need new trains and the tracks need repairing. I don't know where we will be in five year's time; maybe the railways will stop altogether. I hope that private companies will invest in the railways in the future and make them usable again.'

3 Landscape and Climate

Kenya covers an area of 582,646 sq km, more than twice the size of neighbouring Uganda, but smaller than Tanzania, which covers 945,000 sq km. Kenya has some of the most dramatic and beautiful landscapes in the world. Each has its own climate, ranging from the cold, snow-capped peak of Mount Kenya to the hot and humid beaches of the Indian Ocean coast.

The Great Rift Valley

Cutting across Kenya from north to south is the Great Rift Valley. The valley was formed as fault lines in the Earth's surface moved apart, causing the land between them to slowly sink. The valley floor now rests 1,000 m below the escarpment (steep walls) on either side of it. Dotted throughout the valley is a series of shallow lakes that includes Lakes Nakuru and Bogoria, which are famous for attracting flamingos. The flamingos gather on the shores in such vast numbers that the lakes sometimes appear pink from a distance. They are found here because they feed on the algae that thrives in the alkaline water of Nakuru and Bogoria.

▼ Lakes in the Great Rift Valley attract thousands of flamingos.

IN THEIR OWN WORDS

'My name is Kimtac Koyumi and I'm 35 years of age. I live with my family close to Lake Victoria and Kericho. The land here is good for farming, thanks to the hot temperatures that cause water to evaporate from Lake Victoria and fall on our land as regular rainfall. We're still poor, like most farmers in Kenya, but the good land and climate means we can grow some tomatoes and other vegetables to sell in the market. We have even been able to buy a plough and now I can earn money by ploughing people's land for them.'

The high temperatures in the Great Rift Valley mean that water evaporates rapidly, leaving behind minerals and salts that make the water more alkaline than normal.

▼ *White sands and blue seas on Kenya's Indian Ocean coast.*

The coastal strip

Kenya's 540 km of beautiful Indian Ocean coastline has a hot and humid climate where temperatures remain between 24 and 28°C throughout the year. Combined with the palm-fringed beaches, mangrove swamps and spectacular coral reefs, the Kenyan coast is a true tropical paradise. Many of the million or so tourists who visit Kenya each year will spend time in the coastal resorts around Mombasa.

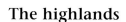
The highlands

Either side of the Great Rift Valley lie mountain chains that reach heights of between 3,000 and 4,000 m. The highest peaks are Mount Elgon on the Uganda border (4,321 m) and Mount Kenya or 'Kirinyaga' as it is known locally. At 5,199 m, Mt Kenya is the second highest mountain in Africa. Although it stands on the equator, its summit is high enough to be covered in snow all year round.

▲ *Kenya's highlands are the most fertile area in the country.*

The highlands of Kenya are cooler than elsewhere and have more regular rainfall. This means they are well-suited to growing crops and much of the best farmland is found here. The western edge of the Great Rift Valley is especially fertile and most of Kenya's valuable tea is grown in this region.

The lowlands

Large sections of Kenya lie below 1,000 m and it is here that Kenya's famous savannah grasslands such as the Masai Mara

◄ *The dry lowlands of the north are best suited to pastoralism.*

and Tsavo are found. Tsavo is the biggest, but the Masai Mara is more popular with visitors who come to see its enormous herds of mammals. Between June and July up to two million animals arrive in the Masai Mara to feed on the fresh grasses that sprout up following Kenya's rains. These fall mainly between March and May, with a shorter rainy season between late October and December.

Most of Kenya receives relatively little rainfall, and is known as an arid or semi-arid environment. This is particularly true of the northern lowlands that cover around two-thirds of the country. Here, rainfall is too low for crops to grow and the main economic activity is pastoralism (the keeping of livestock). In the far north only camels can survive the extreme, desert-like conditions.

▲ *Topi, one of many species of mammal found in the Masai Mara.*

IN THEIR OWN WORDS

'My name is Sirus and I am now 15 years old. I am a member of the Pokot people and we live in a very hot part of Kenya. The climate is too dry to rely on crops and so we keep cattle instead and travel with them to find fodder and water. There have been many droughts in this area and our cattle have died. I'm now undergoing the Pokot rites of passage into adulthood. We wear traditional dress made from animal skins and live in the bush for three months. The older men come to teach us about how to live in such a dry land. They're very wise.'

Natural Resources

Energy resources

With a lack of its own fossil fuels such as coal, gas or oil, Kenya must rely on expensive imports for its energy. Oil is Kenya's primary fuel import and makes up around 15 per cent of its total import costs. Imported oil is refined in Mombasa. Kenya then resells some of its refined oil to neighbouring countries such as Uganda and the Democratic Republic of Congo.

To reduce its reliance on imported oil, Kenya has been developing hydroelectric power (HEP) over the past few decades. In 1998 HEP produced around 80 per cent of Kenya's electricity. New dams being built at several locations mean that HEP will become increasingly important to Kenya over the next decade and reduce the need for Kenya to import more oil to meet its energy requirements.

Despite the growth in electricity generation in Kenya, most Kenyans still rely on wood or charcoal as their main source of energy for cooking and heating. This is especially true in rural areas that are beyond the reach of the electricity network. Some rural schools and hospitals have solar panels to provide electricity and as it becomes cheaper, the use of solar technology is growing.

▶ *Turkwel Gorge is Kenya's biggest dam. It should produce about 15 per cent of Kenya's electricity, but low rainfall means it has never been fully operational.*

An underground resource

In Kenya's Rift Valley, the heat of the earth is used to generate geothermal energy in the form of electricity. Volcanic activity taking place underground causes water to boil into super-heated steam and force its way to the surface. When the steam is captured and piped to a power station, it can be used to turn turbines and generate electricity. The Olkaria geothermal power station near Naivasha produces about 8 per cent of Kenya's electricity in this way and in 2001 construction began on a second power station at the same site.

▲ A vent releases excess steam at Olkaria geothermal power station.

IN THEIR OWN WORDS

'My name is Jack Ogwang and I'm a construction worker here at the Olkaria geothermal power station. The steam comes from the ground and is taken by pipes to the power station where it generates electricity. My job is to fit the pipes for carrying the super-hot steam. I helped build the first power station here in 1981-2 and we're now building a second one. Geothermal power doesn't produce polluting emissions like oil-fired power stations, so it's better for the environment. As geothermal power develops, Kenya may be able to close some of its polluting, oil-powered stations.'

A rich land

Under careful management, the highlands of Kenya are among the most fertile and productive farmland in Africa. This area produces some of Kenya's most valuable exports including tea, coffee and sugar, as well as locally used crops such as maize. The land also supports the forests that provide the majority of Kenyans with the materials used to build their houses and with fuel for cooking and heating.

▶ *Beans are one of several crops grown by Kenyan farmers for export.*

IN THEIR OWN WORDS

'I'm Pauline Matinguong and I'm now 68 years old, too old for collecting wood. My grandson, Ronald, helps me lift the wood to the side of the road and then I wait to sell it to passers by. I collect the wood from the forests around here, but over the years they've been shrinking as people clear them for land. Collecting wood is hard work, but I've done it since I was a small child. I will probably die collecting wood, but it is my only source of energy and income so I have little choice. I hope that electricity will reach these parts some day so that my grandson's generation don't have to collect wood. That would save time and help to protect the environment.'

Lacking in minerals

Kenya has no major reserves of minerals such as oil, gold or diamonds. Where minerals are found, they are found only in small quantities. For example, gold is found in northern Kenya and panned by local people. Limestone is one of the few minerals Kenya has in any great quantity. This is mined at several locations and used to make cement for Kenya's construction industry.

◀ *Limestone quarries can be found throughout much of Kenya.*

Soapstone

One of the most unusual minerals mined in Kenya is soapstone. This is a soft stone found in various colours and often with a beautiful grainy pattern, similar to that found in wood. It can be easily carved and made into objects, from simple plates and bowls to detailed sculptures. Soapstone is one of the most popular materials for making tourist souvenirs, but is only found in Kenya in the Kisii district near Lake Victoria.

Soda ash

Kenya's most valuable mineral is the soda ash mined at Lake Magadi near the Tanzanian border. Soda ash is used in many industrial processes, including the manufacture of paper, glass and soaps. During the 1990s Kenya developed fluorite mining in the Kerio valley, north of Eldoret. Fluorite is used in the steel, chemical and ceramic industries.

◀ *The soda ash pools and factory near Lake Magadi.*

Fishing

Although Kenya's share of Lake Victoria is smaller than that of Uganda and Tanzania, the lake is heavily used for fishing. Nile perch and Tilapia are caught and exported to Europe and the Middle East and are also eaten locally, along with several other types of fish. Fish catches grew from around 100,000 tonnes in 1979 to more than 500,000 tonnes in the early 1990s. However, in recent years fish stocks have been falling because of over-fishing. New regulations, such as limits on the size of fishing nets, have been introduced to protect Kenya's fish resources for future generations.

▲ *Few people have fridges in Kenya, so fish must be dried for storage. This woman is preparing fish for sale at market.*

Wildlife as a resource

Wildlife is not often thought of as a resource, but in Kenya it is of great economic importance. In the past, wildlife provided local people with food, clothing and medicines. Today this is less common, but wildlife has become an important attraction for tourists. National parks have been set up to protect native animals, and the parks earn valuable income from the many thousands of people who visit them each year.

◀ *A male lion is a top attraction for tourists visiting Kenya's spectacular national parks.*

When the parks were first established, there was some resistance from local people who had traditionally used the land in the new parks for farming or herding their livestock. They felt frustrated that they were banned from the land, yet did not share in the profits of tourism. Around Amboseli National Park, the Maasai people even began to kill wildlife in protest. However, since the late 1980s the national parks have worked more closely with local people to make sure that they benefit from tourism. In this way wildlife has become a valuable resource and is protected by local people.

▲ *Wildlife is considered an important economic resource in Kenya today.*

IN THEIR OWN WORDS

'I'm Catherine Wekesa and I'm a warden for Kenya Wildlife Service (KWS). Ever since I was young I've been interested in wildlife. After college I studied wildlife management and I've worked with the Kenya Wildlife Service for thirteen years now. If we don't take care of wildlife today, we'll be talking about it as the new dinosaurs tomorrow. Here at Hell's Gate National Park, we're working with local landowners to develop the park further and to protect wildlife. We want to open campsites and nature trails. Because of the lack of big cats such as lions and leopards, it's safe to walk and cycle in this park. Most of all though, we need more tourists to fund our development.'

5 The Changing Environment

One of the greatest challenges facing Kenya is the protection of its environment. This is particularly important because so much of Kenya's economy depends on agriculture and wildlife. There are worrying signs that Kenya is beginning to suffer serious environmental degradation, but there are also encouraging examples of conservation and new ideas to help preserve and improve Kenya's urban and rural environments.

Water pollution

Kenya is naturally short of water due to its low rainfall, which is quickly absorbed by the dry ground and plants when it falls. Much of the water it does have is of poor quality because there are few laws protecting water supplies from industrial pollution and most domestic water supplies are untreated.

▲ *Traffic congestion is a problem in several Kenyan cities. It is a major cause of air pollution, which can lead to health problems for urban dwellers.*

IN THEIR OWN WORDS

'My name is Alice and I live near Lake Magadi. In rural areas like this, water supplies are poor. We have to walk very far, maybe five kilometres, to find water. The same water is used for everything: drinking, cooking, watering our animals, bathing and doing laundry like I am today. I know this can make the water dirty and give us disease, but I have no choice. I hope that one day my village will get a borehole or well to improve our water. Many villages now have boreholes supplied by the government or by charities from overseas. The problem is that about half of Kenya suffers like we do, so we could be waiting a long time for a borehole – it is a major problem.'

▲ *Water is a scarce resource in Kenya. These women use Lake Naivasha to do their laundry.*

Agricultural chemicals, factory waste, domestic waste and sewage all find their way into local water supplies. Diseases such as diarrhoea and cholera (caused by contaminated water) are common among local people. Many urban wastes are toxic and can harm wildlife if they enter the water system. For example, during the 1980s and 1990s thousands of flamingos were dying in Nakuru because of metal pollutants entering the lake from nearby factories and a refuse dump. New pollution controls have reduced this problem and in 2001 flamingos began breeding at Nakuru for the first time in sixty-six years.

Urban areas can suffer particularly poor water quality. Basic water and sewage systems are unable to cope with the rapidly growing urban population. The slums that surround Kenya's major cities are the worst affected, as they usually have no sewage system at all. The problem is made worse by the lack of waste collection facilities. Household waste blocks drains, causing them to overflow into the streets and even into people's homes.

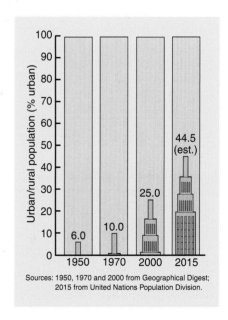

Sources: 1950, 1970 and 2000 from Geographical Digest; 2015 from United Nations Population Division.

▲ *The dramatic rise in the number of Kenyans living in cities has caused serious problems with pollution in urban areas.*

Plastic waste

Plastic bags have added dramatically to the problem of urban waste. Before plastic bags, paper or other natural materials were used for holding goods. Unlike plastic, these would break down over time. Local residents have now taken to burning waste and piles of burning rubbish are a common sight along roadsides. This is not a solution to the waste problem, however, because the rubbish releases toxic smoke and fumes as it burns, creating air pollution.

▲ *Burning litter adds to pollution in most of Kenya's towns.*

Waste recycling

Although Kenya has serious problems with waste management, waste is often recycled in imaginative ways. In urban areas whole communities survive by recycling materials and turning waste into useful products. For example, an old car wheel has many uses: the tyres are made into sandals, the inner tube is cut to make strapping for tying goods together, and the metal centres are used to make a type of stove called a *jiko* (similar to a barbecue). Plastic and glass containers are also re-used and goods are endlessly repaired until they have no further use.

◀ *Many goods, such as these reusable plastic containers, are recycled.*

Environmental improvement

Throughout Kenya there are various projects aimed at improving the environment. The government promotes the teaching of safe waste disposal, for example. It is also working with various organizations to provide safe water

▼ *Turning waste paper into fuel is a positive solution to waste.*

and sanitation facilities. In 1970 only 15 per cent of the population had access to safe water supplies, but by 1999 this had risen to 50 per cent. Many other projects have been started by communities or individuals. The Green Belt Movement is a collection of women's groups who promote the conservation of Kenya's trees. Since 1977, Green Belt members have planted over 12 million trees in Kenya and even beyond.

IN THEIR OWN WORDS

'My name is Peter Macharia and I work for City Garbage Recyclers. We are based in Nairobi and decided that something must be done to deal with the city's rubbish. We use different techniques to recycle rubbish. Our most successful project is our fuel bricks. These are made from old newspapers that are collected and pulped and then mixed with charcoal dust. A special machine squeezes this mixture into a tight brick shape, producing one every eight seconds. When they are dry the bricks make a very efficient fuel, better than wood or charcoal. Nairobi still has a problem with rubbish and it needs more recycling like this.'

Forests under threat

At Independence in 1963, about 30 per cent of Kenya was covered in forest. By 2001 this had fallen to less than 3 per cent. The forests have been cleared to make way for more agricultural land, for use as fuel wood, or as raw materials for the construction and paper industries. In the 1990s deforestation was so severe that it was beginning to cause rivers to dry up. The forests act as a giant sponge, storing rainwater and releasing it into the rivers during the long, dry season. Without the forests, the rivers no longer flow, threatening HEP production, agriculture and drinking-water supplies. In 2001 the government announced plans to clear a further 10 per cent of forests to provide land for the growing population. However, conservationists believe that further deforestation will cause major water shortages and harm more people than it will benefit.

▼ *Trees used for building are one cause of Kenya's shrinking forests.*

IN THEIR OWN WORDS

'My name is Mary Karame and I work here at Bantu Tree Nursery. Like many other nurseries throughout Kenya, we produce seedlings to sell to local people. My job is to encourage people to plant seedlings, which help reduce erosion on the slopes of nearby Mount Kenya. Its slopes have been cleared of trees to grow peas for export, but soil erosion has increased as a result. I hope that, with our help, the slopes of our mountain will again be covered by forests and not just peas for supermarkets in Europe.'

Soil erosion

The roots of trees and other plants help to hold fragile soils together. Without the protection of vegetation, the soil is easily washed away by heavy rains or becomes dust and is blown away on the wind.

Soil erosion is also caused by overgrazing. Livestock strip the ground of its vegetation and their hooves grind the soil into a fine dust. Over time this problem has worsened. As settlements grow and land is used for other activities, pastoralists are forced to tend their animals in ever smaller areas. As a result, their livestock cause increasing damage to the environment. In extreme cases, soil erosion can lead to desertification. This is when the land is so damaged that it becomes desert-like and can no longer support humans or animals.

▼ *Erosion is extremely severe where tree cover has been removed.*

The Changing Population

Population growth

During the 1980s and early 1990s Kenya had one of the fastest growing populations in the world. Its total population increased from just 6.3 million in 1950 to reach 30 million by 2000. The rate of growth has now slowed, but with over half the population under the age of 18, it will continue to grow as these young people have children of their own. It is estimated that Kenya's population will be around 37.6 million by 2015 and increase to over 51 million by 2050.

When populations increase so quickly it is difficult for the government to keep pace in providing facilities such as schools and hospitals. Land also becomes scarce in rural areas, forcing farmers to use less-suitable areas such as steep slopes or forests. Others leave rural areas altogether and move to urban centres in a process known as urbanization. In 1963, less than one in ten people lived in urban areas, but by 2001 one in four people lived in Kenya's sprawling towns and cities. The shortage of housing means many urban residents live in giant slums that surround the city. Mathare Valley slum on the edge of Nairobi is home to some 100,000 people – more than the population of other major towns.

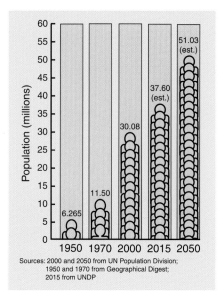

Sources: 2000 and 2050 from UN Population Division; 1950 and 1970 from Geographical Digest; 2015 from UNDP

▲ *The population of Kenya has increased dramatically since 1950 and the growth is predicted to continue.*

◄ *Providing education, housing and health care for Kenya's youthful population is a challenging task.*

IN THEIR OWN WORDS

'I'm Esther and I'm 16 years old. I'm on the far right in this picture. My family are all Samburu, a group of pastoral people similar to the Maasai, and we live close to Mount Kenya. We grow food on our *shamba* (garden) and keep some goats and cattle, but life is hard here because we have a big family. You can see there are six of us here, but there are many more. My three brothers are away with the cattle and we have many relatives to care for. My mother says that when I have a family, I should have fewer children than she has. Unfortunately, it's difficult for us to get health care and plan our families properly. The nearest health centre is a whole day's walk away from here and it rarely has supplies anyway.'

Population distribution

Most of Kenya's population lives in or around the highlands and the more fertile lowlands close to the coast and Lake Victoria. For example, Nyanza province, next to Lake Victoria, covers just 2 per cent of Kenya, but is home to about 17 per cent of the population. In comparison, the arid lands of North East province cover 22 per cent of the country but are home to just 2 per cent of the population.

▶ *Rapid urbanization means many Kenyans live in crowded shanty towns.*

A varied population

Although most Kenyans are black, there are also communities of Asian and white (mainly European) Kenyans. Most Asians and whites settled in Kenya during the period of colonial rule. Asians came mainly from India as workers to help build the railway. When the railway was completed many chose to stay in Kenya, settling in the main towns along the route of the railway, such as Kisumu. Along with the Europeans, Asians own and run many of Kenya's most successful businesses, benefiting from strong trading links with their original countries.

At Independence, Kenya's first president, Jomo Kenyatta, recognized the contribution of Europeans and Asians to the country and encouraged them to stay and work together with the black Africans. This co-operation was known as *harambee*, which means 'pull together' and was a favourite phrase of Jomo Kenyatta's. Today a large number of the white and Asian populations were born in Kenya, and consider themselves entirely Kenyan.

◀ *Many white Kenyans are the descendants of Europeans who first came to Kenya generations ago.*

IN THEIR OWN WORDS

'My name is Jayartilal Shah and I've lived in Kenya all my life. My parents moved to Kenya from India before the Second World War (1939-45). My grandfather came to help the British build the railway from Mombasa in 1897. My family settled here in Nairobi, mostly as shopkeepers. In my shop I sell mainly leather goods, but my business is not doing so well at the moment because the economy is growing slowly and people don't have money to buy things. I have never visited India and I like living in Nairobi. Its mix of local people and the visitors from all over the world make it a very interesting place to live.'

Over 200 languages are spoken amongst the black population of Kenya, which consists of seventy different ethnic groups. Despite their differences, several groups share similar backgrounds and work closely together. Others are quite different and largely excluded from modern day-to-day life. Occasionally different groups fall out over land or other issues, but compared with many African countries Kenya's people live well together.

▶ *These men are Muslims. Islam is one of several religions practised by Kenya's varied population.*

Changes at Home

Growing inequality

Throughout Kenya people experience very different standards of living. In general, the white and Asian populations enjoy a better standard of living than the black population. They tend to live in larger, well-constructed houses in Kenya's main cities and their children benefit from good schools and health care. Many have a higher standard of living than if they lived in Europe or North America.

▲ *Wealthy homes are protected by security fences and often have guards.*

The majority of the black population are much poorer than the white and Asian communities. Most live in low-quality housing that frequently needs rebuilding and the majority live in rural areas. They usually have low incomes and cannot always afford schooling and healthcare for their families. Across Kenya, over a quarter of the population suffer extreme poverty, surviving on less than US$1 per day.

In urban areas, very poor people may beg on the streets or turn to crime in order to survive. In the larger cities this often includes children whose families are unable to support them. During the 1990s the number of children living on the streets increased dramatically as thousands of parents died of HIV/AIDS. In 2000 there were over half a million 'AIDS orphans' in Kenya.

▶ *Poverty in Kenya is greatest among the black population.*

IN THEIR OWN WORDS

'My name is Lonzio and I'm 12 years old. As you can see I'm working hard to collect water to help my mother. Like many Kenyans, we're very poor, so I can't afford to go to school. I did go for a while, but it was too expensive. My mother was very sad for me to leave, because she says education can help us beat poverty. I have written to my uncle in Eldoret to see if he can sponsor me to return to school. If he can't help then I might try and get a sponsor from overseas, but that can be very difficult. My mother tells me about people who are educated and now have good jobs and live well. It's hard for me to imagine that.'

There are exceptions to these patterns of inequality. Some black Kenyans have become extremely wealthy since independence. Most of them benefit from powerful connections and are from the same Kikuyu or Kalenjin tribes as many government members. Over the last few decades the government has often helped its own relatives and communities instead of those who most need help. This sort of corruption has been blamed for the continued poverty suffered by so many Kenyans.

▶ *A minority of black Kenyans now enjoy a high standard of living.*

◄ *This classroom is far better-equipped than many in Kenya. Some schools are a single room in a simple tin or earthen building with no windows and few facilities.*

Education

Poverty is not only about a lack of money. It is also about a lack of basic services such as education. Education is especially important as it gives people the skills and knowledge to find better-paid jobs. In Kenya tuition is free for all children until the end of primary school, but parents have to buy books and uniforms and pay fees to maintain the school buildings. This means many parents can't afford to educate their children. In 1999-2000, there were some 2.5 million Kenyan children who were not attending school.

Women's roles

Women are often among the worst affected by poverty. This is because of their role as household providers. For example, it is often a woman's job to provide water for the family. In much of Kenya women may have to walk several kilometres to find water and then carry the heavy load home again. This is not only tiring, but also time-consuming, which means it can prevent women from doing income-earning activities. In areas where new wells have been dug to

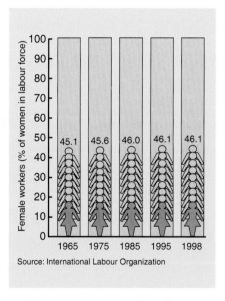

▲ *The percentage of Kenyan women who do paid work has increased only slightly since 1965.*

provide water supplies, women's lives have improved dramatically. Many of them have used the saved time to earn an income, which benefits the whole family.

When educated, women are also better able to care for the health of their family. Because they can read and write they are able to take advantage of new opportunities such as women's credit groups. These offer small loans for women to set up their own businesses, but often require them to keep written records of how the money is used.

▲ *Collecting firewood is one of the many tasks women do.*

IN THEIR OWN WORDS

'My name is Grace and like many women in Kenya I have to work very hard. I'm expected to do the work around the home, care for my family, and find paid work to help earn money. This is sometimes called the triple burden of women and it means we work much harder than men, and for longer hours. It's only midday, but I've already collected water and firewood for my home, given my children breakfast and taken our goats to the pasture. Now I'm trying to sell some of our tomatoes to earn some money to buy cooking oil and rice. I don't want my daughters to suffer work like I do, which is why I work hard to send them to school. With an education they can find a good job in the city and escape a hard life.'

Healthcare

Kenya's healthcare system suffers from a serious lack of funds. For each 100,000 people Kenya has only fifteen doctors, compared to 164 in the UK and 245 in the USA. Although about 75 per cent of Kenya's population live in rural areas, around 80 per cent of Kenya's doctors are based at health centres in cities. New clinics are beginning to open in the countryside, but for many people traditional medicine using plants and local healers is still the cheapest and closest type of health care available to them.

The HIV/AIDS problem

Kenya's first AIDS case was reported in 1986 and since then the disease has spread to all corners of the country. At the beginning of 2000, an estimated 14 per cent of the adult population were infected with HIV, the virus

▲ *Frequent check-ups help to improve children's health, but for many Kenyans health centres are too far away to visit regularly.*

▼ *This is a march to warn people about the dangers of HIV/AIDS.*

that causes AIDS. In addition an estimated 78,000 children under 15 years of age were infected with the virus. The HIV virus has spread rapidly because the use of condoms during sex, to prevent infection, is very low in Kenya. Children are often infected by their mothers during pregnancy, birth or breast-feeding.

In 2000 the government began to describe HIV/AIDS as a national disaster. Over 500 people were dying every day and the average life expectancy fell by six years during the 1990s, to just 51 by the year 2000.

The government is working hard to educate people about HIV/AIDS. Education is particularly important because many Kenyans do not fully understand how HIV/AIDS is transmitted, so schools now teach children about the disease. A similar scheme in neighbouring Uganda has been very successful in raising awareness of HIV/AIDS and reducing infection rates.

▲ *Many AIDS orphans are forced to beg to earn a living.*

IN THEIR OWN WORDS

'My name is Gilbert and I'm standing on the far left in this photo. I'm helping to promote awareness about HIV and AIDS, or *ukimwi* as it is called here. The disease is a major problem for us and many people are being infected and dying. I have lost many of my friends and I'm only 23 years old. Ukimwi can infect anyone; it does not choose its victims. I work with all of Kenya's people to educate them about avoiding infection. There are posters on billboards and in offices, on farms and in factories informing people about HIV/AIDS. We use drama and workshops to teach people about safe sex and health care.
It will be a long, hard battle, but the government is now helping us to fight it. We will win, we have to win!'

Religion

The local church or mosque is often at the centre of village or town life in Kenya. Christianity is the largest religion and is practised by about two thirds of the population. Many people became Christians when missionaries from Europe settled in Kenya during the colonial period. Missionaries still often help to fund schools and health centres in Kenya. About 6 per cent of Kenyans are Muslims and over a quarter of Kenyans still follow traditional beliefs, but, like many traditions, such beliefs are now declining.

▼ *Christianity has replaced traditional beliefs across much of Kenya. Here Maasai people are waiting to attend church.*

Loss of tradition

One of the most striking changes in Kenyan home life has been the loss of traditional beliefs and customs. This change has been so rapid that many urban Kenyans have more in common with people living in North America or Europe than with their grandparents' generation. Their music is heavily influenced by Euro-American pop, they eat western-style fast foods and they like to buy items such as CDs and mobile phones.

IN THEIR OWN WORDS

'My name is Rosemary and I'm 25 years old. I live in Mombasa where I work as a hairdresser. I'm married, but do not have any children yet. My parents think I should be having many children because it's part of our traditional life. I don't think they like me working in the city and I know they don't like my modern clothes and hairstyles. My husband doesn't mind. He works in a bank and we enjoy the same things, like pop music, the cinema and eating in restaurants. I'm not very interested in my traditions; I prefer the modern life I have now.'

In rural areas traditional life remains stronger, particularly among the elderly. In the most remote areas many customs such as rites of passage into adulthood are still practised. Among the Pokot people, for example, young boys are sent to live in the bush for three months where they learn skills such as hunting and looking after their livestock.

In some parts of Kenya traditional cultures are preserved as a tourist attraction. In many of Kenya's safari lodges, Maasai dancers are brought in to perform for guests. Some people don't like the idea of presenting local traditions as entertainment, while others point out that without the interest of tourists, some traditional customs could be lost for ever.

▶ *A Kikuyu elder wearing traditional dress is now a rare sight.*

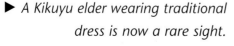

Pastoralists

One group of people whose lifestyle has remained very traditional is Kenya's pastoralist communities. These include the Maasai, Samburu and Turkana people. Pastoralists earn their living from their livestock and may travel great distances to find food and water for their animals.

Some pastoralists spend days or weeks living away from their families with their livestock. They build temporary shelters from materials such as branches and animal hides. Their lifestyle means they have few possessions, as these would be difficult to carry. Many still carry spears, or more recently guns, to protect their livestock from wild animals or cattle raids from neighbouring tribes. In recent years, some pastoralists have begun to settle and turn to other activities, because their local environment can no longer support so many people and livestock. In northern Kenya, for example, many Turkana pastoralists have taken up fishing on Lake Turkana. Despite these changes, most pastoral communities maintain their traditions by keeping some livestock (especially cattle) as they are a sign of wealth and power within their culture.

▼ *Pastoral lifestyles remain common, existing side by side with the modern world.*

Improving urban homes

One of Kenya's greatest challenges is to improve the lives of its growing urban population. Slum residents endure some of the worst poverty of all Kenyans, generally suffering from more disease, pollution and crime. The government is working with other organizations to improve conditions by providing basic facilities. These are known as site and service schemes. The government supplies water, sewage and electricity to an area, leaving local people to build the housing themselves. Streetlights are installed on some schemes, which helps to improve security.

▲ New sewers, such as the one being constructed above, help improve the quality of urban homes.

IN THEIR OWN WORDS

'I'm Paul Aosa and I originally come from Kisii, near Kisumu, but like many people I moved to Nairobi. I came to study sociology at the university here and have since worked as a social worker in Nairobi's urban slums. The slums are a real problem because people just keep coming from the country to live here and find work. There is no housing or services for them and unemployment is high. They are forced to build homes in the slums. I am trying to help people improve their living conditions, but the ten slums I work in have nearly a million people – it is a near impossible task! I am encouraging people to work together to build drainage ditches or to save up and pay for a borehole to be installed.'

8

Changes at Work

Globalization

Like most countries, Kenya is adapting to a more global economy in which its companies are having to compete with those from all over the world to sell their goods in a global market. The government is making it easier for foreign companies to invest in Kenya. In time this investment will mean the creation of more jobs for the Kenyan people.

Telecommunications

The rapid development of telecommunications such as mobile phones and the internet is helping Kenya to compete in the global economy. Kenyan companies can attract new customers using the Internet or use it to assist their business. For example, Kenyan flower growers use the Internet to receive orders from the companies they supply in Europe. By attracting more business, telecommunications are creating new jobs in Kenya and encouraging the teaching of skills needed to operate and maintain the new systems.

▲ *Mobile phone use is growing rapidly among wealthier Kenyans.*

◀ *Improved communications help attract businesses to invest in Kenya.*

Tourism

In the mid-1990s tourism accounted for almost a fifth of Kenya's income. However, following a period of political turmoil, the number of visitors fell in 1997 and 1998. In 1997, violent riots occurred around the Mombasa resorts during the presidential elections. Then, in August 1998, 263 people were killed when terrorists bombed the US embassy in Nairobi. Since then, Kenya has been working hard on projects that will hopefully revive tourism.

Several of these projects are 'eco-tourism' projects. They are intended to benefit local communities and cause minimal disruption to the natural environment. They range from community-led wildlife sanctuaries to coral diving. As interest in such activities grows, it is hoped that eco-tourism will help more Kenyans secure more jobs in tourism.

▲ *Tourism is of great importance to the economy, especially around Mombasa, on Kenya's coast.*

IN THEIR OWN WORDS

'My name is Kerichon and I'm a cook here in Il Ngwesi community conservation project. We opened a small lodge here in 1995 and welcome visitors who come to see the special wildlife such as the rare Grevy's Zebra and rhinos that live on our Maasai reserve. We have learned that the wildlife is very valuable and helps us earn a good income from tourism. I have even given up some of my cattle. Cattle can die, but we can earn money all year from tourism and use the profits to invest in our community. Our education and health has improved greatly. We've won many awards for our sustainable tourism and there are now several other projects like ours opening in this area.'

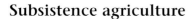

Subsistence agriculture

About 80 per cent of Kenyans work in agriculture and many more depend on the land for their survival. Most Kenyans living in rural areas are subsistence farmers, using their crops and livestock primarily to feed their families. Today, most people also grow some crops for sale in the rural markets that take place daily throughout Kenya. Others grow crops for specific buyers. In western Kenya for example, farmers grow sugar cane or tea that they then sell to the big factories for processing and export. The money they earn is used to purchase goods they cannot produce themselves or to pay for services such as school or health care fees.

Unemployment

A shortage of suitable land means that many people are being forced to leave rural areas to look for paid work. Some jobs are available on large estates, such as the tea

▼ *Few rural farmers can afford an ox and plough. Most work is done by hand.*

IN THEIR OWN WORDS

'My name is Joseph Gishira and I live near Nakuru on my one-acre farm. This land is all I have and I must farm it with my family to provide food for us to eat or to sell if we need money. We grow maize to make *ugali*, our local food, and beans and potatoes. I also grow napier grass to feed my two cows. I earn some money from my seven pear trees by selling the fruit on the roadside. This is seasonal though, and in a bad year my family has very little money at all. Things are so much more expensive than they used to be and it is difficult to earn enough from farming alone. I will encourage my children to get paid jobs if they can find them.'

plantations or flower farms, but there are too few to go around. Many people head to the towns in search of employment, but there are limited opportunities, especially for unskilled workers. As a result, there is a large unemployment problem in Kenya. In 1998, it was estimated that about half of the workforce were officially unemployed. Given the slow growth of the Kenyan economy in recent years, unemployment is unlikely to improve in the near future. The government will need to encourage more companies to invest in Kenya if it is to create more jobs.

▶ *These people are part of a local group that trains people to make crafts for tourists.*

Informal work

Commercial agriculture and tourism may be the most important parts of Kenya's economy in terms of earnings, but the informal sector is vital to the smooth running of the economy. The informal economy is made up of people with locally useful skills. They provide cheap goods for local consumption, such as furniture, pots and pans, or tools. They also provide local services such as cobblers, tailors, hairdressers and mechanics.

For many years the government considered the informal sector a problem because earnings could not be taxed. More recently, the government has realized that important skills are learnt in the informal economy and that it supports the formal sector. It is now working with Kenyan banks to help workers in the informal sector develop their businesses. Workers can apply for loans that will help move their business into the formal economy. In turn, the government can collect taxes that allow it to invest more in services and development projects.

▲ *Food vendors are part of the important informal economy.*

New opportunities

Kenya's economy must continue to take advantage of new opportunities if it is to support its growing population. In 1999 Kenya joined Tanzania and Uganda in forming the East African Community (EAC). This organization aims to

▼ *Women bring surplus crops to sell at market.*

IN THEIR OWN WORDS

'My name is Peter Owino and I'm 14 years old. I live here in Kwa-Muhua, near Naivasha, with my uncle. He is training me to be a blacksmith and bicycle repairer. My parents have little money and so I was forced to leave school and look for work, but without skills it's very hard. One day I hope to buy a bicycle of my own and use it to transport charcoal to market. I am learning to make the racks for carrying charcoal and the sellers tell me they make good money in the markets. Eventually I could use the skills I am learning to be a mechanic. Kenya needs more mechanics because our vehicles are old and are always breaking down on the bumpy roads.'

promote closer trade links and co-operation between the three economies. As the strongest economy, Kenya should find the agreement particularly beneficial as it begins to trade its products with Tanzania and Uganda. But if Kenya is to thrive in the twenty-first century, it must move away from its heavy dependence on agriculture and tourism and develop other profitable industries.

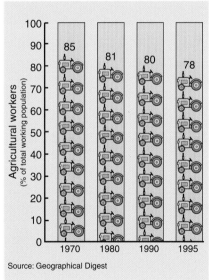

100 90 **85** 80 **81** **80** **78** 70 60 50 40 30 20 10 0
1970 1980 1990 1995

Agricultural workers (% of total working population)

Source: Geographical Digest

▲ *The percentage of Kenyans working in agriculture has fallen since 1970, but remains high.*

◀ *The Trans-African highway links Kenya to neighbouring Tanzania and Uganda.*

9

The Way Ahead

Much to do

Kenya has changed in many positive ways since it became independent in 1963. Its people are healthier and better educated, and it has maintained peace in a region where many countries have not. But Kenya still has much to do. Over half its people still live in poverty, its environment is under increasing pressure from human activity, and it is having to adjust to its role in a more global and hi-tech economy.

Obstacles to progress

Several obstacles stand in the way of Kenya's continuing development. HIV/AIDS continues to affect more and more Kenyans every day. Poverty is perhaps the most far-reaching problem, leading to ill-health, lowering education levels and depriving people of a sense of hope for the future. Tackling poverty would solve many of Kenya's problems. To do this, the people and the government must work together to put an

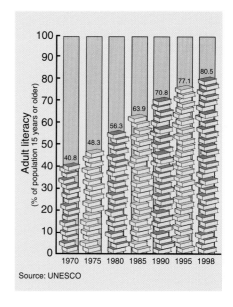

Source: UNESCO

▲ The increase in the number of adult Kenyans who can read and write shows that opportunities for education are increasing in Kenya.

◄ There is much to be done if these young footballers are going to have a chance to break the cycle of poverty.

end to corruption, so that all Kenyans can share the wealth of their country. Reducing corruption would also attract foreign investment. New industries could be established, providing jobs and greater economic security.

Positive signs

Although there are challenges ahead, many Kenyans are already fulfilling the potential of this beautiful land. Eco-tourist projects have won world prizes, hi-tech farms are revolutionizing agriculture, community groups are developing new businesses, and the spirit of *harambee* – pulling together – remains strong.

▶ *The Kenyatta tower, built to celebrate independence, remains a positive symbol.*

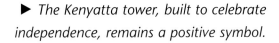

IN THEIR OWN WORDS

'I'm Cathleen Nyagah and today I'm graduating in Business Studies and English from Maseno University in Kisumu. Our president awarded me my degree and my family came to watch. My degree is a good sign for Kenya. The future looks bright for all of us who work hard enough. Soon I hope there will be education for everyone in Kenya, so that all of those who want to can obtain degrees – especially girls. Without education our chances of building a successful country are not so good. For me, though, I think the future will be good!'

Glossary

Agriculture Farming to grow food and other plants for human use.

Alkaline A substance which, when dissolved in water, has a pH of over 7. It is the opposite of acidic.

Ancestors Members of your family who lived in the past.

Cash crops Crops grown to sell or export for money. They include tea, coffee, flowers, sugar cane and fruits.

Colonial Period when a country was occupied and ruled by another country. Kenya, for example, was a colonial territory of Britain until 1963.

Corruption Describes behaviour that is dishonest or unfair. Often related to governments and money.

Culture The beliefs, customs, language and behaviour shared by a group of people. It may include certain foods, music, art, clothes and stories.

Descendants People related to those who lived in the past. For example, you are a descendant of your grandparents.

Desertification A condition whereby soils lose their fertility and so create an area that is similar to desert.

Economy The system of income and expense, employment and production in a country.

Eco-tourism Tourism developments that are carefully managed to ensure that local communities benefit and visitors cause minimal environmental disruption.

Evaporation The process whereby water is converted to a gas or vapour.

Export To sell goods to another country.

Faults Fractures or breaks in the rocks of the earth's crust (outermost shell of the earth).

Formal economy The part of the economy that is made up of industries, businesses and workers who pay taxes to the government and whose profits contribute to their country's GDP.

GDP Gross Domestic Product (GDP) is the monetary value of goods and services produced by a country in a single year. Often measured per person (capita) as 'GDP per capita'.

Geothermal energy The use of super-heated steam from deep underground to drive turbines for generating electricity.

Great Rift Valley A steep-sided valley between 30 and 100 km wide, formed by land sinking between faults in the earth's surface (crust). The Great Rift Valley stretches from Mozambique in the south to Syria in the north and passes through Kenya.

HIV/AIDS Human Immunodeficiency Virus (HIV) is a deadly virus spread via unprotected sex, and contaminated needles or blood supplies. It can develop into Acquired Immuno-Deficiency Syndrome (AIDS), which is fatal. Expensive drugs can keep people alive, but there is as yet no cure.

Hydro-electric power (HEP) Electricity generated by water as it passes through turbines. These normally involve large dams across river valleys that form artificial lakes behind them.

Import To buy goods from another country.

Independence When a country is self-governing. Kenya gained its independence from Britain in 1963.

Informal economy The part of the economy that is made up of workers whose activities and income are difficult to tax. Though not included in the country's GDP, their work is important to the local economy.

Mineral A naturally occurring rock or substance.

Panning The washing of earth or sediment, using a pan (similar to a wok) in the hope of finding gold.

Pastoralists People who depend primarily on livestock (especially cattle) for their livelihoods.

Population The total number of people in a place at a given time.

Sanitation The provision of hygienic toilet and washing conditions to prevent the spread of diseases associated with human waste.

Savannah A dry-land ecosystem dominated by tropical grassland with scattered trees and bushes.

Slums Makeshift settlements close to urban centres that normally lack basic services and are often built illegally.

Soil erosion The removal of soil naturally (by water or wind) or by humans by poor agricultural practices, deforestation or overgrazing.

Subsistence Agriculture farming that provides food mainly for the household. Surplus food may be sold.

Urbanization A process whereby the people of a region or country move from rural areas to settle in towns and cities.

Further Information

Books to read

Country Studies: Kenya by Heather Blades (Heinemann Library, 2000)

Countries of the World: Kenya by Rob Bowden (Evans Brothers, 2002)

Kenya: Promised Land? by Geoff Sayer (Oxfam Publications, 1998)

World Fact Files: East Africa by Rob Bowden and Tony Binns (Hodder Wayland, 1998)

World Focus: Kenya by David Marshall and Geoff Sayer (Heinemann Library, 1994)

Websites

www.kenyaweb.com
A general website for information on Kenya, organized by subject. Includes daily news headlines.

www.kenyatourism.org
The Kenya Tourist Board website contains all the information you would need to arrange a visit to Kenya.

www.kenya-wildlife-service.org
Contains information about Kenya's national parks, its wildlife and the latest conservation and project news.

www.oxfam.org.uk/coolplanet/ kidsweb/world/Kenya/kenhome
Oxfam's 'cool planet' website has a special section focussing on Kenya and Oxfam's work there.

Useful addresses

Kenya High Commission
45 Portland Place
London W1B 1AS
Tel: 020 7636 2371
Email: kcom45@aol.com
Website: http://www.kenyahighcommission.com

Kenya Tourist Office
25 Brooks Mews
London W1Y 1LF
Tel: 020 7355 3144
Email: info@kenyatourism.org
Website: http://kenyatourism.org

Oxfam
274 Banbury Road
Oxford OX2 7DX
Tel: 020 7355 3144
Email: oxfam@oxfam.org.uk
Website: http://www.oxfam.org.uk

Survival International
11-15 Emerald Street
London WC1N 3QL
Tel: 020 7242 1444
Email: info@survival-international.org
Website: http://www.survival-international.org

World Wide Fund for Nature (WWF)
Panda House
Weyside Park
Surrey GU7 1XR
Tel: 01483 426 444
Email: info@wwf.org.uk
Website: http://www.wwf.org.uk